Best
Traditional Creole and Cajun
Recipes from
New Orleans

Dedicated to my family.

Introduction:

What do you think of when you think of New Orleans? If you are like me, you think of food! New Orleans, Louisiana is known for a lot of things: Mardi Gras, Jazz Festival, Riverboats, Bourbon Street and lot of rich, flavorful food dishes that are specific to just that one city. There is both Creole and Cajun style dishes and I like them both. After spending over three years in New Orleans and taking several cooking classes on the cuisine I have written this recipe book with some of my favorite dishes. I hope that you enjoy!

Appetizers

Oysters Rockefeller

Ingredients:

2 slices bacon
24 unopened, fresh, live medium oysters
1 1/2 cups cooked spinach
1/3 cup bread crumbs
1/4 cup chopped green onions
1 tablespoon chopped fresh parsley
1/2 teaspoon salt
1 dash hot pepper sauce
3 tablespoons extra virgin olive oil
1 teaspoon anise flavored liqueur
4 cups kosher salt

Directions:

1. Preheat oven to 450 degrees F (220 degrees C).
2. Cook the bacon, drain, crumble and set aside.
3. Clean oysters and place in a large stockpot.
4. Pour in enough water to cover oysters.
5. Bring to a boil.
6. Remove from heat and drain and cool oysters.
7. When cooled break the top shell off of each oyster.
8. Using a food processor, chop the bacon, spinach, bread crumbs, green onions, and parsley.
9. Add the salt, hot sauce, olive oil and anise-flavored liqueur and process until finely chopped but not pureed (about 10 seconds).
10. Arrange the oysters in their half shells on a pan with kosher salt.
11. Spoon some of the spinach mixture on each oyster.
12. Bake 10 minutes until cooked through, then change the oven's setting to broil and broil until browned on top.
13. Serve hot and enjoy!

Red Beans and Rice

Ingredients:

1 pound dry kidney beans
1/4 cup olive oil
1 large onion, chopped
1 green bell pepper, chopped
2 tablespoons minced garlic
2 stalks celery, chopped
6 cups water
2 bay leaves
1/2 teaspoon cayenne pepper
1 teaspoon dried thyme
1/4 teaspoon dried sage
1 tablespoon dried parsley
1 teaspoon Cajun seasoning
1 pound andouille sausage, sliced
4 cups water
    2 cups long grain white rice

Directions:
1. Rinse beans, and then soak in a large pot of water overnight.
2. In a skillet, heat oil over medium heat.
3. Cook onion, bell pepper, garlic, and celery in olive oil for 3 to 4 minutes.
4. Rinse beans, and transfer to a large pot with 6 cups water.
5. Stir cooked vegetables into beans.
6. Season with bay leaves, cayenne pepper, thyme, sage, parsley, and Cajun seasoning. Bring to a boil, and then reduce heat to medium-low.
7. Simmer for 2 1/2 hours.
8. Stir sausage into beans, and continue to simmer for 30 minutes.
9. Meanwhile, prepare the rice. In a saucepan, bring water and rice to a boil.
10. Reduce heat, cover, and simmer for 20 minutes.
11. Serve over white rice and enjoy!

Shrimp Remoulade

Ingredients:

¾ cup chopped celery
¾ cup chopped scallions (white and green parts)
½ cup chopped curly parsley
1 cup chopped yellow onion
½ cup ketchup
½ cup tomato purée
½ cup Creole mustard or any coarse, grainy brown mustard
2 tablespoons prepared horseradish, or to taste
¼ cup red wine vinegar
2 tablespoons Spanish hot paprika
1 teaspoon Worcestershire sauce
½ cup salad oil
4 dozen jumbo (15 count) shrimp, peeled, boiled, and chilled
1 small head of iceberg lettuce, washed, dried and cut into thin ribbons

Directions:

1. Mince the celery, scallions, parsley, and onions in a food processor.
2. Add the ketchup, tomato puree, Creole mustard, horseradish, red wine vinegar, paprika, and Worcestershire.
3. Begin processing again and add the oil in a slow drizzle to emulsify.
4. Stop when the dressing is smooth.
5. Chill for 6 to 8 hours or overnight.
6. Correct the seasoning with additional horseradish, if desired.
7. In a large mixing bowl, add the sauce to the shrimp and toss gently to coat.
8. Serve on top of a bed of lettuce and enjoy!

Oysters Bienville

Ingredients:

24 oysters in shells
Coarse rock salt
1/2 cup finely chopped green onions
1 clove garlic, minced
3 tablespoons butter or margarine
1/3 cup all-purpose flour
1/4 teaspoon salt
1/4 teaspoon ground white pepper
1/4 teaspoon ground red pepper
1 cup chicken broth
1/2 cup whipping cream
3 beaten egg yolks
1/2 pound cooked, shelled shrimp, chopped
1/2 cup finely chopped fresh mushrooms
2 tablespoons dry white wine
1/4 cup grated Parmesan cheese
2 tablespoons fine dry bread crumbs
1/8 teaspoon paprika

Directions:

1. Open oysters in shells.
2. Remove oysters from shells with a knife and drain well.
3. Wash shells.
4. Place each oyster in the deep half of each shell.
5. Arrange on a bed of coarse rock salt in shallow pans or on crumpled tin foil
6. In a saucepan cook green onions and garlic in butter or margarine (about 5 minutes) or until tender.
7. Stir in flour, salt, white pepper, and red pepper.
8. Add chicken broth and cream, stirring until well blended.
9. Cook and stir over medium heat until the mixture is thickened and bubbly.
10. Reduce heat.
11. Gradually stir about half of mixture into beaten yolks.
12. Return mixture to saucepan.
13. Bring to a gentle boil.
14. Cook and stir 2 minutes more.
15. Stir in shrimp, mushrooms, and wine.
16. Heat through.
17. Remove from heat.
18. Spoon 2 tablespoons of the shrimp mixture over each oyster.
19. Combine Parmesan cheese, bread crumbs, and paprika.
20. Sprinkle over oysters.
21. Bake in a 400 degree F oven for 15 to 20 minutes or until golden on top and the oysters curl.

Soups

Crawfish Bisque

Ingredients:

1/2 cup butter
1/2 cup chopped onion
1/2 cup chopped green onion
1 pound crawfish tails
2 (10.75 ounce) cans cream of potato soup
1 (10.75 ounce) can cream of mushroom soup
1 (15 ounce) can yellow corn, drained
1 (14 ounce) can white corn, drained
1 (8 ounce) package cream cheese
1 pint half-and-half
3 tablespoons Creole seasoning
Salt and ground black pepper to taste

Directions:

1. Melt butter in a large pot over medium heat. Cook and stir chopped onion and green onion in melted butter until softened, about 5 minutes. Add crawfish tails, potato soup, mushroom soup, yellow corn, white corn, and cream cheese. Cook and stir until cheese melts completely into mixture. Pour half-and-half into the pot; stir.
   Season with Creole seasoning, salt, and black pepper. Cook until hot, about 15 minutes.

Shrimp Gumbo

Ingredients

2 tablespoons vegetable oil
2 tablespoons all-purpose flour
2 pounds medium shrimp, peeled and deveined
2 tablespoons vegetable oil
3 cups chopped okra
2 onions, chopped
1 (14.5 ounce) can diced tomatoes
2 quarts water
1 bay leaf
3 cloves garlic, minced
1 teaspoon salt
1 red bell pepper, chopped
Ground black pepper to taste

Directions:

1. In a large skillet over high heat, add 2 tablespoons oil and flour to the pan, and whisk together quickly.
2. Continue cooking and stirring until a dark roux forms.
3. Stir in shrimp.
4. Cook and stir for a few minutes, until the shrimp turns pink.
5. Set aside.
6. In another pan, heat 2 tablespoons oil over medium heat.
7. Stir in okra and onions; cook until okra is tender.
8. Mix in tomatoes.
9. Add water, bay leaf, garlic, salt, red pepper, and the shrimp mixture.
10. Cover, and cook slowly for 30 minutes.
11. Serve and enjoy!

Creole Turtle Soup

Ingredients:

1 Cup Unsalted Butter for roux
1/2 Cup All Purpose Flour for roux
4 Tbsp. Unsalted Butter
1 pound Turtle Meat Cut into 1/2 inch cubes
1 1/2 Cup Onion, Finely Diced
1 Cup Celery, Finely Diced
1/4 Cup Green Onion, Finely Sliced
2 tsp Garlic, Minced
2 Fresh Bay Leaves
1 1/2 Cup Fresh Tomato, Diced
4 cups Beef Stock
1 Pinch Cayenne
1 Pinch Ground Allspice
2 tablespoons Fresh Thyme Leaves
1 tablespoons chopped marjoram
Salt and Black Pepper to taste
1/4 Cup Fresh Lemon Juice
4 tablespoons Worcestershire Sauce
3 tablespoons sherry
3 Hard Boiled Eggs, whites diced, yolks riced
Lemon Slices
5 tsp chopped parsley

Directions:

1. Melt the 1 Cup of Butter in a heavy bottomed saucepan.
2. Whisk in the flour, cook to make a tan colored Roux.
3. Set aside.
4. In a large saucepan, melt 4 tablespoons of unsalted butter over medium-high heat.
5. Add the diced Turtle Meat and sauté until nicely browned.
6. Lower the heat to medium, add both types of onions, the celery, and garlic.
7. Season with salt and black pepper. Sauté until the vegetables are tender.
8. Add the tomatoes.
9. Season with a little salt so they will break down.
10. Cook for 10 minutes.
11. Add the beef stock, Worcestershire, cayenne, allspice, and bay leaves.
12. Bring to a boil, then down to a simmer.
13. Simmer for 20-30 minutes, stirring occasionally and skimming off any impurities that may rise to the surface.
14. Whisk in the roux.
15. Simmer until thickened and smooth. Add the thyme, and marjoram, simmer for 15-20 minutes more.
16. Add the lemon juice, 3 teaspoons of parsley, and the riced egg yolk.
17. Heat through.
18. Serve and enjoy!

Main Dishes

Jambalaya

Ingredients:

2 tablespoons butter
1 pound chicken breast, cut into bite-sized pieces
½ pound andouille sausage, sliced in ¼ inch slices
1 yellow onion, chopped
3 cloves garlic, minced
1 green bell pepper, diced
1 stalk celery, diced
1 cup white long grain rice
1 (14.5 ounce) can diced tomatoes
2 tablespoons Creole seasoning (see recipe below)
1-2 teaspoons hot sauce
1 teaspoon Worcestershire sauce
2 cups chicken broth
2 bay leaves
¾ teaspoon salt
½ pound medium raw shrimp, deveined (optional: tails removed)
4 green onions, thinly sliced

Creole Seasoning Ingredients:

2 teaspoons garlic powder
2 teaspoons onion powder
2 teaspoons sweet paprika powder
1½ teaspoons dried thyme
1 teaspoon dried oregano
1 teaspoon dried basil
1 teaspoon cayenne pepper
¾ teaspoon salt
½ teaspoon freshly ground black pepper

Directions:

1. Make the Creole seasoning by combining all the spices in a coffee or spice grinder and grind in to a fine powder.
2. Place the chicken in a bowl with 1 tablespoon of the Creole seasoning.
3. Set aside.
4. Heat the butter in a skillet and brown the chicken on all sides.
5. Add the andouille sausage and cook for another 3 minutes or so until the sausage begins to brown.
6. Add the onion, garlic, celery, and bell pepper and cook for 3-4 minutes. A
7. Add the rice, diced tomatoes and remaining tablespoon of Creole seasoning, hot sauce, Worcestershire sauce, salt and pepper and stir to combine. Add the chicken broth and bay leaves.
8. Bring it to a boil, reduce the heat to medium-low, cover and simmer for 15 minutes, giving it one stir around the halfway point. Add the shrimp, cover, and simmer for another 10 minutes or until the rice is tender.
9. Serve sprinkled with some sliced green onions.

Crawfish Etouffee

Ingredients:

1 lb. Louisiana crawfish tails
3-5 cloves of garlic, minced
1 large onion, diced
1 green bell pepper, diced
1 red bell pepper, diced
2-3 celery stalks, diced
2 tbsp. canola oil
2 tbsp. butter
4 tbsp. flour
2 teaspoons Cajun seasoning
3-4 scallions, chopped
Rice

Directions:

1. In a cast iron skillet, heat the oil.
2. Add the butter.
3. When the butter has melted and mixed up into the oil, add the flour.
4. Stir the flour constantly to avoid burning to make a roux.
5. When the roux is a nice tan color, toss in the vegetables and sauté until the onions are translucent.
6. Peel the crawfish tails.
7. Put the crawfish tails in a bowl and add 1.5 cups of water.
8. Stir the tails around in the water to get the juices.
9. Strain the tails from the juice, and set them aside.
10. Cook down the vegetables and then add the crawfish juice to the pan.
11. Bring to a boil.
12. Add the Cajun seasoning.
13. Bring it to a boil then lower to a simmer and cook for 20 minutes.
14. Add the crawfish and scallions.
15. Stir
16. Cook about 5 minutes.
17. Serve over rice and enjoy!

Oyster Po-Boy

A Po-Boy is a submarine sandwich with various types of fillings. One of the most popular in New Orleans is the Oyster Po-Boy.

How the sandwich got its name is widely debated. One story says that during a 1929 streetcar workers strike, a restaurant owner gave the people on the picket line free sandwiches. Another story is that the name is derived from the French phrase Pour Boise which means "for drink." And still, a third story says that the original recipe for the sandwich came from the Great Depression when restaurants would make sandwiches from whatever they had on hand, scraped together and served as a sandwich.

Whatever its origins, the Po-Boy is a delicious traditional New Orleans dish which I'm sure that you will enjoy. I have included the recipe for the Oyster Po-Boy below.

Ingredients:

1/2 cup mayonnaise
1 1/4 teaspoons minced canned chipotle chilies
1/2 teaspoon fresh lemon juice
6 cups vegetable oil
1 large egg
1/4 cup whole milk
2 1/2 teaspoons salt
1 1/2 cups cornmeal
1/4 teaspoon black pepper
2 cups shucked oysters, drained (about 36)
Bread loves for sandwiches
Shredded lettuce

Directions:

1. Whisk together mayonnaise, chipotle, and lemon juice in a bowl.
2. Cover bowl with plastic wrap and chill.
3. Heat oil in a deep heavy pot over high heat to fry the oysters.
4. Whisk together egg, milk, and 1 teaspoon salt in a bowl.
5. Mix cornmeal, 1 1/2 teaspoons salt, and pepper in a flat bowl until well combined.
6. Dip oysters one at a time, first in egg mixture and then in cornmeal mixture, coating well.
7. Carefully put coated oysters in the hot oil, and fry, turning occasionally, until golden and cooked through, (about 1 to 2 minutes)
8. Transfer the oysters with a slotted spoon to paper towels to drain.
9. Cut the bread loaf in half to open the sandwich.
10. Spread the chipotle mayonnaise on each half of the bread.
11. Add lettuce.
12. Add the oysters. Close and enjoy!

Muffuletta

A muffuletta is a traditional New Orleans sandwich made with cured deli meats and a tapenade spread, served on an Italian loaf bread.

Ingredients

5 ounces pimento-stuffed olives (1 cup), sliced, plus 2 tablespoons of liquid from the jar
6 ounces chopped giardiniera (pickled Italian vegetables) (1 cup), plus 1 tablespoon of liquid from the jar
2 tablespoons drained capers, plus 2 teaspoons of liquid from the jar
3 ounces pitted Calamata olives (1/2 cup), sliced
2 1/2 teaspoons minced garlic
1 tablespoon minced shallot
1 teaspoon dried oregano
1 teaspoon dried parsley
Pinch of dried thyme
Pinch of crushed red pepper
1/2 cup extra-virgin olive oil
1 large loaf seeded Italian bread, split
1/4 pound sliced fresh mozzarella
6 ounces sliced capocollo or prosciutto
1/4 pound sliced Genoa salami
1/4 pound sliced mortadella
1/4 pound sliced mild provolone cheese

Directions:

1. In a medium bowl, stir the pimento-stuffed olives with the giardiniera, capers and their respective liquids.
2. Add the Calamata olives, garlic, shallot, oregano, parsley, thyme and crushed red pepper.
3. Stir in the olive oil and let the mixture stand for 1 hour.
4. 2Open the Italian bread.
5. Spoon the olive salad on both sides of the bread and spread evenly.
6. Arrange the mozzarella slices on the bottom half of the bread, then top with the capocollo, Genoa salami and mortadella.
7. Arrange the provolone cheese on the top half of the bread, covering the olive salad completely.
8. Carefully close the sandwich.
9. Wrap the sandwich tightly in plastic and let stand for 30 minutes or up to 2 hours.
10. Cut the sandwich into 8 pieces.
11. Serve and enjoy!

Shrimp Creole

Ingredients

4 ounces (1 stick) unsalted butter
2 cups chopped onions
1 cup chopped green bell pepper
1 cup chopped celery
1 teaspoon salt
1/2 teaspoon cayenne pepper
2 bay leaves
one 14.5-ounce can diced tomatoes
1 tablespoon chopped garlic
1 teaspoon Worcestershire Sauce
1 teaspoon hot sauce, or to taste
2 tablespoons all-purpose flour
1 cup water
1 cup shrimp stock
2 1/2 pounds peeled and deveined large shrimp
1 tablespoon Emeril's Essence Creole Seasoning
1/2 cup chopped green onions
2 tablespoons chopped parsley
4 cups cooked long-grain white rice

Directions:

1. In a large sauce pan, over medium heat, melt the butter.
2. Add the onions, peppers, and celery to the pan.
3. Season the vegetables with salt and cayenne.
4. Sauté the vegetables until they are wilted, about 6 to 8 minutes.
5. Stir in the bay leaves, tomatoes, and garlic.
6. Bring the mixture to a boil and reduce to a simmer.
7. Continue to cook for 15 minutes.
8. In a small bowl whisk the flour and water together and add the mixture to the tomatoes.
9. Cook for 4 to 5 minutes.

10. Add the shrimp stock, Worcestershire and hot sauce and continue to cook for 10 minutes longer. Season the shrimp with Essence and add them to the pot. Cook the shrimp until they are pink and cooked through (about 6 to 7 minutes).
11. Stir in the green onions and parsley.
12. Serve with white rice.

Louisiana Alligator Creole Stew

Ingredients:

4 lbs. Louisiana Alligator
1 inch cubes
3 Tbsp. canola oil
4 Tbsp. minced garlic
2 cups diced onions
1 1/2 cups diced green bell peppers
1 cup diced celery
1 cup white wine
5 cups chicken stock
1 48 oz. can diced tomatoes
3 cups potatoes, medium dice
2 Tbsp. thyme, dried
2 Tbsp. oregano, dried
2 bay leaves
1/4 tsp. cayenne
2 tsp. Tabasco sauce
1 tsp. Worcestershire sauce
Salt, to taste
Pepper, to taste
1/4 lb. Butter
2 cups green onions, chopped
2 French baguette, sliced and toasted

Directions:

1. Heat canola oil in a pot over medium-high heat.
2. Add garlic, onions, green peppers and celery.
3. Cook for 6-8 minutes, until onions are translucent and vegetables are tender.
4. Add white wine, chicken stock, canned tomatoes, potatoes, thyme, oregano, bay leaves, cayenne, Tabasco and Worcestershire.
5. Season to taste with salt and pepper.
6. Bring to simmer and cook for 5 minutes.
7. Add Louisiana Alligator to stew.
8. Cover and simmer for 45 minutes.

9. Add butter and green onions to stew and stir until melted.
10. Remove bay leaves.
11. Serve with sliced toasted French bread.

Desserts

Beignets

Ingredients:

2 1/4 teaspoons active dry yeast
1 1/2 cups warm water (110 degrees F/45 degrees C)
1/2 cup white sugar
1 teaspoon salt
2 eggs
1 cup evaporated milk
7 cups all-purpose flour
1/4 cup shortening
1 quart vegetable oil for frying
1/4 cup confectioners' sugar

Directions:

1. In a large bowl, dissolve yeast in warm water.
2. Add sugar, salt, eggs, evaporated milk, and blend well.
3. Mix in 4 cups of the flour and beat until smooth.
4. Add the shortening, and then the remaining 3 cups of flour.
5. Cover and chill for up to 24 hours.
6. Roll out dough 1/8 inch thick.
7. Cut into 2 1/2 inch squares.
8. Fry in 360 degree F hot oil.
9. If beignets do not pop up, oil is not hot enough.
10. Drain onto paper towels.
11. Shake confectioners' sugar on hot beignets.
12. Serve warm.

Mardi Gras King Cake

The King Cake is served during the Mardi Gras festivities. It is a ring cake that is colored the traditional colors of Mardi Gras: Green, Purple and Gold. Often a small plastic toy is baked in to the cake and the person that finds the toy is given an honor, prize or has to throw the next party.

Cake Ingredients:

1 (16-ounce) container sour cream
1/3 cup sugar
1/4 cup butter
1 teaspoon salt
2 (1/4-ounce) envelopes active dry yeast
1/2 cup warm water (100° to 110°)
1 tablespoon sugar
2 large eggs, lightly beaten
6 to 6 1/2 cups bread flour*
1/3 cup butter, softened
1/2 cup sugar
1 1/2 teaspoons ground cinnamon

Glaze Ingredients:

3 cups powdered sugar
3 tablespoons butter, melted
2 tablespoons fresh lemon juice
1/4 teaspoon vanilla extract
2 to 4 tablespoons milk

Glaze Directions:

13. Stir together first 4 ingredients.
14. Stir in 2 tablespoons milk, adding additional milk, 1 teaspoon at a time, until spreading consistency.
15. Sprinkle with purple, green, and gold-tinted sparkling sugar sprinkles.

King Cake Directions:

1. Cook first 4 ingredients in a medium saucepan over low heat, stirring often, until butter melts.
2. Set aside, and cool mixture to 100 degrees F to 110 degrees F.
3. Stir together yeast, 1/2 cup warm water, and 1 tablespoon sugar in a 1-cup glass measuring cup.
4. Let stand 5 minutes.
5. Beat sour cream mixture, yeast mixture, eggs, and 2 cups flour at medium speed with a standing mixer until smooth.
6. Reduce speed to low, and gradually add enough remaining flour (4 to 4 1/2 cups) until a soft dough forms.
7. Put dough on a lightly floured surface and knead until smooth and elastic (about 10 minutes).
8. Place in a well-greased bowl, turning to grease top.
9. Cover and let rise in a warm place (85 degrees F), for about 1 hour or until dough is doubled in bulk.
10. Punch down dough, and divide in half.
11. Roll each portion into a 22" x 12" rectangle.
12. Spread 1/3 cup softened butter evenly on each rectangle, leaving a 1" border.
13. Stir together 1/2 cup sugar and cinnamon, and sprinkle evenly over butter on each rectangle.
14. Roll up each dough rectangle, jelly-roll fashion, starting at 1 long side. Place one dough roll, seam side down, on a lightly greased baking sheet.
15. Bring ends of roll together to form an oval ring, moistening and pinching edges together to seal.
16. Repeat with second dough roll.
17. Cover and let rise in a warm place (85 degrees F), 20 to 30 minutes or until doubled in bulk.
18. Bake at 375 degrees F for 14 to 16 minutes or until golden.
19. Slightly cool cakes on pans on wire racks (about 10 minutes).
20. Drizzle Creamy Glaze evenly over warm cakes.
21. Sprinkle with colored sugars in bands of colors for the Mardi Gras colors of green, gold and purple.
22. Let cool completely.

Bananas Foster

The dish was created in 1951 by Paul Blangé at Brennan's in New Orleans, Louisiana. At this time New Orleans was a major hub for the import of bananas from South America. It was named for Richard Foster, the chairman of the New Orleans Crime Commission and a friend of restaurant owner Owen Brennan.

It is still served at a number of restaurants in New Orleans and elsewhere.

Ingredients:

1/4 cup (1/2 stick) butter
1 cup brown sugar
1/2 teaspoon cinnamon
1/4 cup banana liqueur
4 bananas, cut in half lengthwise, then halved
1/4 cup dark rum
4 scoops vanilla ice cream

Directions:

1. Combine the butter, sugar, and cinnamon in a flambé pan or skillet.
2. Place the pan over low heat either on an alcohol burner or on top of the stove, and cook, stirring, until the sugar dissolves.
3. Stir in the banana liqueur, then place the bananas in the pan.
4. When the banana sections soften and begin to brown, carefully add the rum.
5. Continue to cook the sauce until the rum is hot, then tip the pan slightly to ignite the rum.
6. When the flames subside, lift the bananas out of the pan and place four pieces over each portion of ice cream.
7. Generously spoon warm sauce over the top of the ice cream and serve immediately.

Bread Pudding

Ingredients:

1 loaf French bread
1 quart milk
3 eggs
2 cups sugar
2 tablespoons vanilla extract
1 cup raisins
3 tablespoons melted margarine
Whiskey Sauce
1 cup sugar
1/2 cup butter or margarine
1 egg, beaten
2 ounces bourbon whiskey

Directions:

1. Preheat oven to 350 F.
2. Soak the bread in the milk.
3. Crush with hands to make sure milk is soaked through.
4. Add eggs, sugar, vanilla, raisins and stir well.
5. Pour margarine in bottom of heavy baking pan.
6. Add bread mixture, and bake till very firm, approximately 40 minutes.
7. Cool the pudding, cube it and put in individual dessert dishes.
8. When ready to serve, add whiskey sauce and heat under broiler for a few minutes.

Whiskey Sauce:

9. Cream sugar and butter and cook in a double boiler until very hot and well dissolved.
10. Add well-beaten egg and whip very fast so egg doesn't curdle.
11. Cool and add whiskey.

The End

About the Author

Laura Sommers is a loving wife and mother who lives in Baltimore County, Maryland and has a passion for all things domestic especially when it comes to saving money. She has a profitable eBay business and is a couponing addict. She challenges herself to write books that are enriching, enjoyable, and often unconventional.

Other books by Laura Sommers

- Easy to Make Party Dip Recipes: Chips and Dips and Salsa and Whips!
- Super Slimming Vegan Soup Recipes!
- Popcorn Lovers Recipe Book
- Inexpensive Low Carb Recipes
- Recipes for the Zombie Apocalypse: Cooking Meals with Shelf Stable Foods
- Best Traditional Irish Recipes for St. Patrick's Day
- Egg Recipes for People With Backyard Chickens

May all of your meals be a banquet
with good friends and good food.

Made in the USA
Lexington, KY
03 March 2017